THE BOY IN THE SUITCASE

An Investigative True Crime Novel

Linda Davidson

*For the children who weren't heard in time, and
for the people who learned to listen.*

"Attention is the rarest and purest form of generosity."

— SIMONE WEIL

CONTENTS

PREFACE

Some cases refuse to stay quiet.

They linger in archives and margins, in old photographs and half-remembered headlines, waiting for someone to look again— not for spectacle, but for truth. *The Boy in the Suitcase* is one of those cases. At its center is a child whose life ended before it was ever properly recorded, and a question that haunted investigators, journalists, and communities long after the initial shock faded: **How does a child disappear so completely that only death demands attention?**

This book was written with restraint and purpose. It does not seek to shock, nor to compete with the noise that often surrounds true crime. Instead, it follows the record—patiently, carefully—examining what is known, what was missed, and what later science made possible. The investigation unfolded across years, jurisdictions, and evolving forensic standards. It involved moments of urgency and long stretches of silence. It exposed the limits of systems once thought sufficient, and the human cost of those failures.

Where possible, this narrative relies on primary sources: court documents, police files, contemporaneous reporting, and later forensic findings. In places where the record is incomplete, the absence itself is treated as evidence—of neglect, of procedural blind spots, or of an era that lacked the tools we now take for granted. Reconstructions are grounded in corroborated material and identified as such. Speculation is resisted. The victims remain central.

This is an investigative work, but it is also an act of remembrance. The child at the heart of this story was more than a case file, more than a photograph circulated too late. He was a life that deserved recognition long before it received a name, an explanation, or public concern. Telling his story is not about reopening wounds— it is about refusing to let anonymity become the final injustice.

True crime carries responsibility. It demands accuracy, humility, and care for those who can no longer speak for themselves. This book is offered in that spirit: to document, to contextualize, and to ensure that what happened is neither forgotten nor reduced to rumor.

Some stories are uncomfortable precisely because they matter.

This is one of them.

Trigger & Content Notice

This book addresses the death of a child, neglect, and related courtroom proceedings. Graphic detail is avoided; descriptions remain respectful and necessary to the narrative. Reader discretion advised.

Ethical Note

This story is inspired by real investigative practice but remains **fictionalized**: identities are protected; timelines and locations are altered or blended; procedures are depicted accurately in spirit. A fuller ethics statement appears in the Author's Note.

Linda Davidson

PROLOGUE

— The Road That Kept Its Secret

The road was the kind that people forgot existed.

A narrow stretch of cracked asphalt cutting through the endless green of southern Indiana, used mostly by farmers, delivery drivers, and the occasional traveler looking for a shortcut. On most days, the only sound out there was the wind brushing through the trees and the faint hum of cicadas. But on that cold April morning, the silence broke.

A man driving along Spurgeon Road slowed as something bright caught his eye just off the shoulder — a flash of blue against the pale brush. At first, he thought it was trash, maybe an old piece of luggage dumped by someone cleaning out a garage. But something about the way it sat — almost placed, not thrown — made him stop. He stepped out, boots crunching against gravel, the morning air still sharp with spring frost.

He approached, expecting maybe clothes or someone's forgotten possessions. What he found instead would haunt the state for months.

Inside the suitcase was the small, lifeless body of a boy.

There were no notes. No wallet, no tag, no hint of where he came from or who had loved him. Only the suitcase — a cheap, patterned model you could buy at any department store — and the stillness of a child whose story had been erased.

When police arrived, the scene felt almost unreal. Officers taped off the area, investigators moved quietly, and the sky hung heavy with the weight of unspoken questions. Who was he? How long had he been here? Why had no one come looking?

In the following days, that question — *Why isn't anyone missing him?* — echoed louder than any other. The boy became a symbol of every child who slips through cracks, unseen until it's too late. Investigators worked without sleep, forensic teams studied every inch of the suitcase, and communities across the country waited for answers that didn't come quickly enough.

They called him *the boy in the suitcase*, because no one knew his name. For months, that was how the world referred to him — an identity reduced to an object, a mystery, a plea for justice.

But beneath the headlines and police briefings was something quieter, almost sacred: the collective ache of strangers mourning a child they had never met. People sent flowers to the roadside, left stuffed animals, lit candles. They prayed that someone, somewhere, would recognize him.

What they didn't know yet was that this case would unravel one of the most disturbing and heartbreaking stories in recent memory — a story of innocence betrayed, of silence where there should have been protection, and of a community forced to confront how easily a child can disappear in plain sight.

This book is not about sensationalism. It's about remembrance — about giving back to a boy what was taken from him: his name, his story, his humanity.

Because no child should ever be found in a suitcase on a lonely road, waiting for the world to care.

CHAPTER 1 ROADSIDE DISCOVERY

The morning of **April 16, 2022**, began like any other along that quiet southern Indiana backroad. The wind carried the smell of damp earth from the night's rain, and the sun broke through low clouds that clung to the rolling hills of Washington County. It was a Saturday, the kind of day when life slowed down — when people mowed lawns, checked fences, or made their way into town for errands.

For one man, a collector of scrap metal who often drove those rural routes, it was supposed to be another uneventful morning. He was scanning the roadside for tossed-out appliances or old metal when he noticed something strange just beyond the ditch — a **blue hard-shell suitcase**, oddly placed against the brush, its edges still clean despite the mud around it.

It wasn't unusual to see discarded luggage or trash along those roads, but something about this one stopped him. It was too new, too deliberate. Like it hadn't fallen off a car — like it had been *set there*.

Curiosity won. He parked, stepped out, and walked toward it. The morning air was heavy and cool, and the sound of his boots crunching on gravel felt amplified in the stillness. When he reached the suitcase, he hesitated. The zipper was partially open, as if someone had closed it in a hurry.

He bent down, unzipped it, and saw what no one should ever have to see.

A small body. A boy.

He stumbled backward, his breath caught in his throat. For a moment, the world stopped. Then instinct took over — he reached for his phone, hands shaking, and dialed 911. His voice, trembling but urgent, became the first echo in what would soon become one of the most haunting investigations in the state's history.

The Arrival

When the first sheriff's deputy arrived, the man who had made the call was standing near his truck, pale and silent. He pointed toward the suitcase but couldn't bring himself to say the words. The deputy's training kicked in. He radioed dispatch, called for homicide, forensics, and the coroner, then took a long, steadying breath before approaching.

Even after years in law enforcement, nothing prepares you for a sight like that.

Within an hour, the narrow road was sealed off. Crime-scene tape fluttered in the breeze while investigators from the **Indiana State Police** arrived, careful to preserve every inch of soil, every footprint, every trace of evidence. They photographed, measured, and marked. The suitcase was gently lifted, placed into an evidence bag, and secured for transport.

Inside, they found the small boy's body — around five years old, wearing clean clothes, with no immediate signs of trauma visible from the outside. No identification, no personal belongings, no clue to his name or origin.

Someone had gone to great lengths to erase him.

The Investigation Begins

In the command tent set up beside the road, detectives gathered to review what little they had. The location — a remote stretch of Spurgeon Road, surrounded by forest and farmland — suggested that whoever left the suitcase there knew the area well. It wasn't a place you'd find by accident.

One detective studied a map spread across the table. "Whoever did this wanted him to be found — eventually," he said quietly. "Not buried. Not hidden forever. Just… set aside."

The words hung in the air. It was a chilling thought.

They began canvassing the area — knocking on doors of farmhouses, checking nearby trail cameras, asking residents if they'd seen unfamiliar vehicles. A few remembered a car stopped along the road the evening before. Others hadn't seen anything at all. The boy's face, photographed respectfully at the coroner's office, would soon become the image shared with law enforcement agencies across the country.

The Child With No Name

At the **Washington County Coroner's Office**, the child was examined that same afternoon. Investigators estimated his age between five and eight years. He appeared well-nourished, cared for — no signs of long-term neglect or malnourishment. Toxicology and a full autopsy were ordered.

But what struck everyone most was the absence of anything to identify him. No wallet, no papers, no marks, no missing-person reports that fit.

When cases like this happen, investigators begin with the most basic questions: *Where was the suitcase bought? Who sells that model? Are there surveillance cameras in nearby stores?* They took note of the brand — a hard-shell Las Vegas design — and began tracing its retail history. Every clue mattered.

Meanwhile, state police released a public appeal:

"We are seeking the identity of a young boy found deceased in Washington County, Indiana. Anyone with information, please contact our tip line."

The announcement made local headlines that evening, and by the next morning, the story had gone national. News anchors referred to him as *the boy in the suitcase*, a phrase that stuck, painfully simple yet devastatingly descriptive.

It was the kind of mystery that kept people awake at night — not just because of the horror of the act, but because of what it said about society. How could a child this young go unclaimed, unreported, unseen?

Echoes Across the Country

Tips began flooding in. Calls came from across the U.S. — families of missing children, concerned neighbors, strangers convinced they recognized him. Each lead was logged, cross-checked, and painstakingly eliminated. The emotional toll on investigators was immense.

One trooper later said, "It wasn't just another case. Every one of us has a child, a nephew, someone we thought of when we looked at him. We wanted his name as badly as we wanted justice."

The autopsy revealed further details. Though the exact cause of death would take time to determine, it became clear this was no accident. The condition of the body suggested deliberate concealment. Someone had packed him into that suitcase, zipped it shut, and placed it miles from any home.

Detectives built timelines, plotted routes, and looked for anyone who might have purchased that suitcase recently. Retail chains were contacted. Surveillance footage from stores hundreds of miles away was requested. Still, nothing concrete surfaced in those early days.

It was as though the boy had appeared out of thin air.

The Vigil

As the weeks passed without identification, locals created a small memorial at the site where he'd been found. Flowers, teddy bears, handwritten notes. One card read, *You are loved, even if we don't know your name.*

At night, candles flickered beside the road, the glow visible from passing cars. The rural community — not accustomed to national headlines — became a place of quiet pilgrimage. People came, wept, prayed, and left tokens of care for a child they never met.

The media coverage intensified, but the investigators refused to speculate. They stuck to verified facts, protecting the integrity of the case. Behind the scenes, forensic labs worked tirelessly — analyzing DNA, cross-referencing with national databases, and testing the fibers and dirt clinging to the suitcase's wheels.

Weeks turned into months. Still no match. No missing-person report. No family stepping forward.

A Promise in the Dark

That summer, as the investigation stretched on, one detective reportedly made a quiet promise while standing beside the roadside memorial:

"You will not remain a mystery. We'll find your name. We'll tell your story."

And in time, they would.

But the road to that revelation would expose not just a chain of crimes and deceptions — it would reveal the deeper cracks in the systems meant to protect children. Behind the bright suitcase and headlines lay a web of dysfunction, evasion, and silence.

Before long, a lead from hundreds of miles away would begin to unravel the truth — a truth darker and more complicated than anyone could have imagined.

CHAPTER 2 THE CHILD WITH NO NAME

The Night After Discovery

The first night after the discovery was long and sleepless for everyone involved. The suitcase was secured at the state crime lab, and the boy's remains were transported to Indianapolis for a full autopsy scheduled for the following morning. Outside, rain fell steadily, washing away tire tracks and footprints along the roadside—as if the ground itself were erasing whatever clues it could.

Inside the lab, the air was still and clinical. Dr. Elaine Porter, the state's chief forensic pathologist, prepared her workspace with practiced calm. Years in forensic medicine had taught her that some cases announce their gravity immediately. This was one of them.

"He's not a John Doe," she said quietly to her assistant as the paperwork was reviewed. "He's someone's son."

What the Body Revealed

The examination revealed a boy estimated to be around five years old. He was small, but not malnourished. His body showed no obvious signs of external trauma—no gunshot wounds, no stab injuries, no fractures. The absence of visible violence complicated matters. There would be no immediate answers.

Toxicology samples were collected. Internal organs were examined for disease or poisoning. Subtle findings emerged: congestion in the lungs, swelling in the brain. Nothing, however, pointed to a single, definitive cause of death.

Time of death was estimated at several days to a week before discovery. Cool spring temperatures had slowed decomposition, preserving details that spoke quietly but clearly. His teeth were healthy. His hair had been freshly trimmed. His skin showed no signs of prolonged neglect.

He looked cared for.

Someone, somewhere, had taken time with him—at least enough to make him appear loved.

Dr. Porter recorded her findings with professional restraint, but when the examination was complete, she paused. She covered the small body with a white sheet and whispered words meant for no report.

"We'll find your name."

A Suitcase With a History

Back at Indiana State Police headquarters, the investigation accelerated. Photos, timelines, and maps covered a board that filled quickly as detectives followed every available thread. At the center of it all was the suitcase itself—a bright blue model decorated with Las Vegas imagery.

Tracing the suitcase led investigators through import records and retail distribution chains. Identical models had been sold at Walmart and TJ Maxx stores across multiple states in the Midwest and South. A small sticker inside the zipper offered the first tangible lead: a batch number tied to shipments delivered to select locations in Georgia and Kentucky.

It wasn't proof. But it was direction.

Security footage was requested. Hours turned into days as investigators reviewed grainy video—checkout lines, parking lots, faces caught in passing. Any moment, any transaction, could be the one that mattered.

At the same time, forensic analysts began DNA extraction.

A Child No One Reported Missing

The boy's DNA profile was entered into CODIS and NamUs, the national databases for missing and unidentified persons. Investigators waited, expecting at least a partial match.

None came.

The result was devastating. With thousands of open missing-child cases across the country, the absence of a match suggested a far darker truth: no one had reported him missing.

Media attention intensified. Headlines asked the question investigators could not escape—*Who Is the Boy in the Suitcase?* Tips flooded in. Families reached out, clinging to the possibility that answers—any answers—might come.

Lieutenant Matt Hanley felt the weight of the case deeply. He had worked homicide for years, but child cases carved differently. At home, he watched his own son sleep, the same age, the same fragile frame, safe and known.

During a late-night briefing, Hanley addressed his exhausted team.

"If nobody's looking for him," he said, "then we look harder. Somebody knows something. This child came from somewhere."

When the Trail Turned South

With DNA yielding no answers, investigators turned to forensic reconstruction. Working from medical data and anthropological measurements, artists recreated the boy's face—soft features, open eyes, a calm expression designed to help the public imagine him alive.

When the image was released, it carried a simple plea:

Help us give him back his name.

The response was immediate. Vigils were held. Churches prayed. Schools sent letters and stuffed animals. The case no longer belonged only to law enforcement—it belonged to the public.

Then came a detail that shifted everything.

Soil residue on the suitcase wheels did not match Indiana's terrain. Laboratory analysis identified red clay consistent with parts of Georgia. Investigators expanded their search south, quietly coordinating with law enforcement agencies across state lines.

Among dozens of files, one stood out—not a missing child, but a woman with a history of instability and frequent interstate movement. Her last known residence was near a retail location that sold the same suitcase model.

The pieces were beginning to align.

By June, two months after the discovery, a candlelight vigil was held near the roadside memorial. A small white cross stood in the grass, surrounded by flowers and a weathered teddy bear. Children placed pinwheels in the soil as a pastor prayed for truth and restoration.

Later that night, long after the crowd had gone, a detective returned alone. Watching the pinwheels turn in the humid wind, he whispered, "We'll find you. We always do."

He did not yet know that the trail was about to cross state lines —or that the suitcase was not merely a vessel of concealment, but a map leading directly to those who tried to erase the boy's existence.

CHAPTER 3 A CASE BUILT ON ABSENCE

Built on Absence

The deeper investigators dug, the clearer one truth became: this case was not built on evidence. It was built on what wasn't there.

No fingerprints in national databases. No school enrollment. No missing-person report. No medical records. No trace of a life on paper.

That kind of void doesn't happen by accident.

By early May, the task force had rechecked every available listing of missing children across all fifty states. DNA, dental records, fingerprints, and facial reconstruction had been uploaded to every major law-enforcement system.

The result was the same every time.

Nothing.

Detective Matt Hanley stared at the screen one evening, the glow reflecting back at him like an accusation. "He doesn't exist," he said quietly.

Detective Marisol Vega leaned against the doorframe. "Everybody exists somewhere," she replied. "If he's not in the system, someone made sure of it."

That realization landed hard. No school. No doctor. No daycare. No church registry. No government benefits.

The boy's life had been deliberately quiet.

And invisibility leaves almost no trail.

Tracing the Suitcase

With records exhausted, investigators turned back to the one object that had carried the boy into view: the suitcase.

Forensic analysts scraped for anything digital—retail logs, transaction timestamps, toll cameras, gas-station surveillance. The suitcase's batch code traced back to a warehouse in Georgia, narrowing distribution to a small number of retail locations.

Days of footage followed. Then, finally, something usable.

A woman in her mid-thirties. Sunglasses. A baseball cap. Buying the same suitcase model. The timestamp placed the purchase roughly six weeks before the boy's estimated death.

She paid cash. No loyalty card. But her phone pinged a nearby cell tower.

Analysts cross-referenced the data and isolated a prepaid number —unregistered, recently activated. Call logs showed activity in Louisville, Kentucky and Atlanta, Georgia.

The suitcase had given them a place to start.

The phone hinted at where she went next.

The Southern Corridor

Detectives mapped the route. It cut through the South like a scar— interstates connecting small towns, budget motels, and rest stops where anonymity was easy to maintain.

Hanley and Vega drove it themselves, beginning in Georgia. They visited thrift stores, pawn shops, gas stations—anywhere the suitcase might have appeared again.

In the backroom footage of one store, they saw her more clearly. This time, she wasn't alone.

A child stood beside her. About the right age. Small. Quiet. Holding onto her sleeve.

It wasn't definitive. No facial recognition match. No name.

But it was no longer coincidence.

They had found their first living trace.

The Paper Orphan

Back at headquarters, analysts compiled what they called *The Paper Orphan* report.

It documented how children vanish without ever being reported missing. Families move frequently. Guardians pull children out of school under the guise of homeschooling and never file paperwork. Some are running from debt, addiction, warrants, or custody disputes. Others simply disappear from oversight entirely.

Children like that don't fall through cracks.

They are never recorded in the first place.

Detective Vega studied the report in silence before saying, "He wasn't lost. He was erased."

The words stayed with Hanley. He pictured the reconstructed face—the soft eyes, the careful haircut. A child without records, without presence, without protection.

And someone had zipped him inside a suitcase to make sure he stayed that way.

A Crack in the Silence

The break came in pieces.

Soil analysis confirmed the red clay embedded in the suitcase wheels matched a specific stretch of highway near the Georgia–Alabama border. Teams canvassed rest stops and roadside motels along that corridor.

At one small inn, a clerk remembered a woman checking in under a false name weeks before the discovery. She had a child with her. Quiet. Polite. Carrying a small stuffed dinosaur.

Security footage confirmed the sighting.

Exit footage showed the woman leaving alone.

Days later, the tip line rang. A woman said she recognized the boy's composite sketch from television. "He looks like my neighbor's grandson," she said. "But I haven't seen that little boy in months. The grandmother moved away real sudden."

The address she gave matched the alias used at the motel.

By afternoon, warrants were drafted.

The apartment they entered was empty—but not erased. Crayon drawings on the refrigerator. A toy truck missing a wheel. A child's unmade bed. In the trash, a gas receipt dated two weeks before the body was found. On the back, a child's looping scribble—possibly his name.

"This is all that's left of his handwriting," Vega whispered.

Hanley shook his head. "Not anymore. We've got a trail now."

Back at headquarters, the board finally told a story: suitcase purchase, motel footage, phone pings, gas receipt, red clay. Not answers—but direction.

The silence around the boy had been cultivated. His disappearance planned, not accidental.

As Hanley turned off the lights that night, the map glowed faintly behind him—roads stretching back toward Georgia, toward red clay, toward the truth waiting just beyond reach.

CHAPTER 4 THE SUITCASE SPEAKS

The Suitcase Speaks

From the moment the suitcase was sealed in evidence storage, everyone on the team knew it was more than an accessory to the crime.

It was a witness—mute, but eloquent. Somewhere within its scratches, seams, and soil lay the truth that no one had yet spoken aloud.

Opening the Evidence

Inside the Indiana State Forensic Laboratory, technicians worked in silence. The blue hard-shell suitcase, now empty, rested on a clean stainless-steel table beneath bright white lights. Every inch of it was photographed before a single swab was taken.

Technician Elena Morrow guided a gloved hand along the zipper, collecting microscopic debris. "We treat it like a diary," she told a trainee. "Every surface tells you where it's been and what it's seen."

Fibers, hairs, skin cells—anything that might still cling to the fabric—were lifted carefully and sealed in microtubes. On the base, beneath the wheel casing, they found reddish dust and small grains of quartz mixed with clay. It was the same composition previously flagged by soil analysts: southern red clay, common to Georgia and Alabama.

That match wasn't just symbolic. It narrowed the window of the boy's final journey to a defined corridor of road—a silent trail the suitcase had carried back with it.

The Tag That Wasn't

When the case first arrived, investigators noted the absence of any airline tags or stickers. But under ultraviolet light, faint adhesive residue appeared—the kind left by a removed baggage tag. A chemical developer brought out two partial barcodes and three faded letters:

ATL.

Atlanta.

That single clue changed the direction of the case. If the suitcase had once passed through Hartsfield–Jackson Airport, the perpetrator may have flown recently or reused luggage from earlier travel. Either way, the object was now whispering fragments of a timeline.

Technicians cross-checked flight manifest data for recent one-way tickets purchased in cash between Georgia and Kentucky within a two-month window. It was a long shot, but one manifest contained a name matching an alias found later on a motel receipt from the earlier search.

The suitcase was beginning to tell its story.

Threads and Traces

Forensic fiber analysis turned up several distinct threads caught beneath the zipper teeth—one navy polyester strand and one fine white cotton fiber. Under the microscope, both were consistent with low-cost motel bedding.

"That puts him somewhere indoors before death," Elena noted in her report. "Not outdoors, not transient—somewhere with sheets."

Combined with the motel clerk's earlier statement, it strengthened the theory that the child had spent his final nights in temporary lodging. Investigators returned to the motel chain, retrieving more footage from locations along the southern corridor.

In a facility near Montgomery, Alabama, a camera above the lobby captured a blurry sequence: a woman dragging a blue suitcase toward the elevator at 2:14 a.m. She looked directly into the camera for half a second. The timestamp aligned within forty-eight hours of when analysts believed the boy had died.

When Hanley saw the still frame, he simply said, "The suitcase just spoke."

Days later, another clue emerged. During re-examination, a technician noticed a tiny tear in the inner lining near the wheel mount. Inside was a thin, crumpled piece of paper—small enough to have been overlooked the first time.

It was part of a printed motel receipt, half burned at the edges. The visible text read *Thank you for staying*— followed by a partial ZIP code corresponding to a region just outside Birmingham, Alabama.

Vega traced the zip to a budget motel off the interstate. Management confirmed that months earlier, a guest using an out-of-state ID had checked in with a child but left without notice. Surveillance footage—mostly corrupted—yielded one usable clip: a child walking beside a woman down the hallway, clutching a stuffed dinosaur. The date stamp read March 29.

The boy had lived here.

He had walked these halls.

Now the suitcase wasn't just evidence—it was a bridge between states, timelines, and truths.

The Microscopic Witness

The lab's final revelation came from the most overlooked detail: air.

A sample captured when the suitcase was sealed revealed high concentrations of detergent vapor and faint traces of pine cleaner —chemical signatures typical of industrial janitorial products.

"Someone tried to wash it," Elena concluded. "Not just wipe it— wash it."

That explained the faint scent of bleach noticed during the initial discovery. The suitcase had been scrubbed, dried, and resealed. But chemical cleaning leaves fingerprints of its own—unique combinations traceable to specific brands.

The lab matched the profile to a cleaning solution sold primarily to motels in the same Alabama corridor. Combined with fiber evidence and soil traces, it placed the suitcase—and the crime— squarely in that region within days of the boy's death.

When Hanley reviewed the full report, he read aloud:

"Fibers consistent with motel bedding… soil indicative of Georgia clay… adhesive residue matching ATL airport barcode…"

To anyone else, they were technical details. To him, they were movement. A route. A desperate attempt to erase a child.

"He was moved three times," Hanley said. "Georgia, Alabama, Kentucky, then here."

"And each move left a fingerprint," Vega replied.

She wrote on the whiteboard in red marker:

THE SUITCASE SPEAKS — WE LISTEN.

The Weight of Objects

The next press conference shifted the search south. Images of the suitcase, the composite sketch, and the motel hallway footage aired side by side. Tips came in—fewer, but sharper.

A retired motel housekeeper recognized the suitcase immediately. "I cleaned that room," she said. "The woman left early. She had a boy. He looked tired."

That testimony helped secure interstate warrants. The walls were closing in.

Back in evidence storage, the suitcase sat sealed on its shelf, its once-bright surface dulled by time. Vega visited it one last time before transfer to federal archives.

"People think monsters hide in shadows," she said quietly. "But sometimes they hide behind ordinary things."

She rested her hand on the shell.

"We heard you," she said. "We'll make them hear you too."

The next phase would bring confrontation and reckoning. But this chapter—the chapter of the suitcase—would remain unforgettable.

Because in a case built on absence, it was an object that spoke loudest.

Objects can't lie.

They can only wait for someone to listen.

CHAPTER 5 DIGITAL FOOTPRINTS & DOORBELLS

When the Quiet Starts Talking

It began with a tower ping.

Not a face, not a name. Just a series of numbers a mile high on a spreadsheet: a prepaid phone, awake for brief intervals, skirting the edges of cell coverage like a shy animal at the tree line. Each ping a breath. Each breath a direction.

The Mosaic

Analyst Priya Rao pinned the first map up in the briefing room. The dots looked random at a glance—Georgia, then Alabama, then a thin scatter north—but randomness has patterns if you stare long enough. The phone came alive near a discount store the night the suitcase was purchased. It slept for two days, then chirped again outside a motel just off the interstate. Then again. Then gone.

Priya drew short lines between the pings with a dry-erase marker. "We're not tracking a person," she said. "We're tracking a habit. Short stays. Cash purchases. Night moves."

Detective Vega leaned forward. "Give me cameras where the phone wakes."

They started to build the mosaic: traffic cams at the on-ramp; a single, grainy still from a toll plaza where the license-plate reader caught part of a plate and a dented rear bumper; a convenience store with an aging DVR that hiccupped every six frames but held a clear reflection of a blue suitcase in the glass of the door as it swung open.

The suitcase again. Always the suitcase.

They knocked on doors in a neighborhood near the motel with the burned receipt—not because they expected witnesses, but because the neighborhood had something else: doorbell cameras.

"We hate these cases," one homeowner said, handing over her login. "We love them, too."

Frame by frame, the team walked a street no one had walked that night: a silver sedan easing down the block; a woman in a hoodie stepping out, dragging the blue case; a small figure beside her, hesitant, staying close.

The child shifted his weight. The woman glanced up once, as if listening to the sky. The camera captured that half-second of her face—tired, clenched—then the door shut.

"Time-stamp says 2:12 a.m.," Priya noted. "Cell ping says 2:13. We have them together."

Hanley straightened. The clip was short, but it did something the case board hadn't yet done: it made the route human.

The Phone Wakes

The prepaid device was a cheap brick, purchased in cash at a corner store two months before the discovery. No registered owner. No billing address. But every call leaves residue.

Priya pulled metadata: two one-minute calls to the same number in Louisville; three unanswered texts from another prepaid handset; a single voicemail left on a number tied to a pay-as-you-go plan registered with a motel's street address.

Nothing screamed a name. Everything whispered a pattern.

They drafted orders for historical cell-site location information. When the returns came in, the lines sharpened.

"She avoids towers by hugging coverage gaps," Priya said. "But people get tired. They call when they're scared."

There it was: a late-night, six-minute call from a patch of highway south of Birmingham to a number in Georgia. The receiving phone was active for just that night, then dark forever.

"Fear call," Vega said.

The triangulation placed the source within three blocks of the apartment where they'd found the child's crayon-scribbled receipt.

The Vehicle

The toll-plaza partial plate—G7-5K—wasn't enough to run. But paired with the dented rear bumper and traffic-cam imagery, the field narrowed.

Sixteen candidates. Nine eliminated in hours. Four garaged and immobile. Two waved from porches as officers verified bumpers.

That left one.

A silver sedan registered to a woman with three change-of-address filings in eighteen months and a county form listing "homeschool" for a child who didn't exist in any education database. The car had been sold off-book two months earlier. The bill of sale listed a first name and a phone number that now resolved to air.

"Find the car," Hanley said. "The car finds the truth."

A patrol officer spotted it idling at a flea market. The buyer paid cash. Didn't ask questions. He remembered the woman selling it behind a fast-food place, tossing a suitcase into the trunk before driving off with a different car.

"What did it look like?" Vega asked.

"Blue. Hard shell. Vegas pictures."

The Corridor Narrows

They worked backward from the sale: parking-lot footage, fuel receipts, loyalty-card pings. A clerk remembered selling bleach and "the strong kind of cleaner."

In the footage, the woman's posture was coiled. No child now. Just the suitcase—heavy—as she slammed the trunk.

"Can we get the second plate?" Priya asked.

The camera missed it by two inches.

Two inches—the distance between knowing and almost.

The Louisville number belonged to a rental with sycamores flaking bark like old paint. The landlord remembered the boy. Quiet. Dino noises. Never spoke.

The doorbell camera across the street caught him once, chasing bubbles. He laughed. The sound didn't travel. It didn't need to.

They pulled trash: mail fragments, a missed clinic card, a list— milk, cereal, soap, tape.

Tape.

The case tightened, not with drama but repetition:

– a geofence warrant

– a rideshare driver who remembered the smell of cleaner

– a pawn ticket for a wiped tablet

– a throwaway email that autofilled two names

No strand alone would hold. Together, they hummed.

"Evidence is quiet," Priya said. "You have to listen close."

The Threshold

They found her two states away, in a weekly-rate suite pretending to be an apartment. Vega and Hanley stood outside with a warrant.

"Ready?"

"No," Vega said, and knocked.

The woman froze in the doorway. The room behind her was too clean.

"We need to talk about a child," Vega said. "We need to talk about a suitcase."

Denial gathered, then collapsed.

"I don't know his name," the woman said. A lie—or the kind of truth people use when the real one burns.

Under the sink: industrial cleaner. Pine wash.

In the closet: a luggage set missing one piece.

"The smallest," Vega said.

Back at the station, a cloud backup restored itself when a seized phone hit a charger. A video appeared.

Thirty seconds.

A boy on a motel bed. Dinosaur in his hands. A voice prompts him to say hi. He lifts the toy and makes the soft roar. Compliance shaped like joy.

"We had enough," Vega said.

"But now a jury will understand," Hanley replied.

Outside, evening settled. A church bell marked the hour.

A message buzzed upstairs—a probable genealogy match.

The child was about to have his name back.

CHAPTER 6 THE AUTOPSY STORY

The Autopsy Room Doesn't Believe in Myth

The room where truth is taken from the body has no patience for myth.

Fluorescent lights. Stainless steel. Paper forms in triplicate. A clock that does not hurry. Here, grief is measured in milliliters and centimeters, reported in passive voice so it won't break the page: *It was observed… It was noted… It is the opinion of the examiner…*

1) Intake and the First Accounting

Dr. Elaine Porter stood at the foot of the table, gloved hands still. "We go slowly," she told the resident, a reminder disguised as instruction. "We honor the life by respecting the evidence."

The boy was small on the steel. Age estimated at five to six. No identifying scars. Fingernails trimmed. Hair recently cut. He looked like a child prepared for school picture day, as if appearance could overrule absence.

Chain of custody was read aloud. Photographs taken—front,

profile, posterior—each angle a petition to history: *Remember him as whole.*

There were no bullet wounds, no stab tracks, no blunt-force fractures radiating through bone like lightning. The violence here, if present, had hidden behind subtler choices.

They began with the exterior—notations of height and weight, skin findings, any abrasions. The boy's body bore faint, scattered bruises in various stages of healing, none catastrophic alone, but together suggesting a life of small impacts. The pattern did not shout. It whispered.

"Bruises can belong to children who play," the resident offered tentatively.

"Or to children who learn not to," Porter said, marking diameter and color on the diagram.

She swabbed the mouth, the nose, each fingernail bed. Fibers came away: white cotton, consistent with budget sheets, and threadlike blue strands the lab would later match to the suitcase's lining.

2) The Open Book and What Anatomy Can't Say

The Y-incision was clean, practiced. Ribs lifted. Organs weighed in sequence, each number called out and recorded—heart, lungs, liver, spleen, kidneys—a litany that reduced miracle to measurement, and yet carried reverence in its precision.

The lungs were heavy for a child his size. Congested. In the airways, frothy fluid. In the sinuses, minor edema. No drowning markers. No gross pneumonia. The signs built toward something less theatrical and more cruel: the quietly lethal physiology of oxygen denied.

The brain, removed with care, showed mild cerebral edema— swelling that does not diagnose on its own but testifies to struggle. No hemorrhages. No skull fractures. The spine intact.

"Toxicology," Porter said, as much to the room as to the resident. "Always ask what the chemistry knows that anatomy won't say."

Blood, vitreous humor, bile: drawn and labeled. A small vial of gastric contents noted, volume measured, placed aside. They would wait for the machines to speak.

3) Negative Space, Microscopy, and the Weight of Time

Days passed. Reports stacked. Some told what wasn't there: no common illicit drugs; no therapeutic levels of medications; no carbon monoxide burden; no ethanol in blood. The absence became its own ontology.

What remained were physiology and circumstance: the lung congestion, the brain swelling, the lack of external catastrophic injury, the setting suggested by fibers and chemical traces. A picture forming from negative space.

The resident hovered over the draft. "We can't say the exact minute," he said, "or the exact mechanism."

"We rarely can," Porter replied. "Mechanism is for physics. Manner is for law. Cause is the bridge we walk with humility."

Slides told an older truth. Under the lens, pulmonary alveoli showed edema, small hemorrhages, and a pattern consistent with hypoxia—starvation of oxygen. There were no large airway obstructions, no foreign bodies, no food lodged to simplify blame. Instead, the histology mirrored a scenario in which breathing had been compromised without dramatic trauma.

The pathologist circled the features with a pencil on the photomicrograph. "He fought for air," she said softly.

Estimating time since death is as much art as science. Temperature curves, lividity patterns, the state of rigor, environmental exposure. In this case, spring cool kept the body in a narrow window. Porter anchored the estimate to a 48–96 hour frame before discovery, knowing defense attorneys hated ranges and juries distrusted precision. Truth lives between those two disappointments.

4) The Report, the Translation, and the Interview That Followed

CAUSE OF DEATH: Complications of asphyxia, with contributory factors under investigation.

MANNER OF DEATH: Homicide.

She did not write "accident." She did not write "undetermined." She had seen too many children where the line blurs and adults hide behind it. The bruising pattern, the forensic context, the concealment in luggage, the cleaning chemicals—all of it argued for intention, or at minimum, culpable disregard that the law names with its own harsh clarity.

When she signed, she paused over the signature block. "We will give him his name," she said again, a ritual now. The resident nodded, newly initiated into a priesthood he hadn't known he'd joined.

Detectives aren't doctors, but they have to be fluent in the body's dialect when the body is the only witness left. Hanley read the report three times. Each pass stripped the clinical of its distance.

"He asphyxiated," he said finally, to the room. "Not drowning. Not chemical. Deprived of air."

Vega absorbed it like weather—inevitable, chilling. "Time window puts him alive in Alabama," she said, pointing at the corridor on the board. "And dead before Kentucky."

Priya traced the pings within that window. "Phone sleeps here," she noted, circling a gap that married the autopsy's estimate. "Then wakes two hours later on the interstate."

Silence settled. Not the helpless kind—the assembling kind. Pieces choosing their neighbors.

With a cause and manner in hand, the interviews sharpened. Words weighed heavier when medical certainty stood behind them.

"You understand," Vega told the woman across the table, "that the manner is homicide."

The woman's eyes flickered—fear, calculation, the somatic math of consequences. "He stopped breathing," she said. "It was an accident."

"Accidents call 911," Vega replied. "Accidents don't buy bleach. Accidents don't drive a child across state lines inside a suitcase."

The tape recorder's red eye watched, patient. The woman's hands twisted. She offered a version calibrated for mercy: he fell asleep; he wouldn't wake; panic; cleaning to fight "the smell of death." The words were rehearsed, but the body tells too: the swallow, the averting gaze, the small flinch when Vega said *boy* instead of *him.*

Hanley slid the autopsy summary forward. "This is what the doctor found," he said. "This is what the body says."

The woman's story didn't survive contact with the page.

5) The Edges of Mercy and What the Body Said

People want villains operatic enough to hate without reflection. The room refused that comfort. The facts drew a narrower, uglier figure—someone ordinary, stressed, evasive, perhaps cruel in small daily ways that add up to catastrophe. A person who cleaned and hid instead of calling for help. The law has a precise name for that, too.

Vega stepped out afterward, stood in the hallway under a framed poster about resilience that felt obscene. She thought of the lung slides, how the body whispers the moment air leaves and doesn't return. In her chest, she felt a protective anger, not loud, but fixed.

"We'll carry him into court," Hanley said beside her.

"Alive," she answered. "We'll carry his story alive."

That afternoon, a call from the genealogy desk: a probable kinship link. An aunt's branch lighting up a century of relatives until it held a single leaf that fit the season and the age. The scientists warned about probabilities. The detectives thanked them for certainties anyway.

With a likely family came history—pediatric records in another state that stopped abruptly, a withdrawn school enrollment never replaced, a pattern of moves. Paper trails don't resurrect the dead, but they refute the notion that he was ever no one.

In the quiet of early evening, Dr. Porter drafted a one-page supplemental opinion, the kind prosecutors read aloud when they want a jury to hear the body speak in a human register.

The findings are consistent with hypoxic injury prior to death. The distribution of bruises, the absence of emergent medical aid, and the postmortem concealment support the classification of homicide. In my medical opinion, this child's death was preventable.

She stopped there. Anything more would be preaching, and the body had already done the sermon.

Word of a "major development" leaked without names. Strangers returned to the roadside, setting out fresh flowers and a new stuffed dinosaur. Someone tucked a note under its arm: *You are not forgotten.*

Vega drove by, not stopping, not wanting to make spectacle of a private grief enacted in public. The pinwheels turned in a wind that smelled like rain. She imagined air filling small lungs, imagined the triumphant ordinary act of breathing. The simplest thing in the world. The first right.

In court, months later, a pathologist would explain in simple words what the report had etched in Latin and caution. Jurors would lean forward without knowing they were doing it. Someone would cry softly. Someone would look down at their hands. The defense would ask about ranges, about possibilities, about pathologies that can mimic. The doctor would concede uncertainty at the edges and stand firm in the center.

Because the body had spoken.

It had said: *I was a child. I needed air. I did not receive it. And when I did not, no one called for help. After, I was hidden.*

Medicine is not poetry. But sometimes it rhymes with justice.

CHAPTER 7 THE CIRCLE NARROWS

When the Circle Tightens

The longer an investigation runs, the smaller its world becomes. What starts as a map of half a continent eventually contracts to a single room, a single name, a single truth no one can dodge anymore.

The Wall of Faces

The task-force office had changed. The photographs and receipts and maps were no longer scattered in confusion; they now formed a pattern that radiated inward like a whirlpool. Every line of yarn, every timestamped image, led to one woman—and, increasingly, to the people who had helped her vanish.

Detective Vega pinned a new photo to the center board: a still frame from an ATM camera. The woman's hood was down, her face half-lit by the machine's glow. She was withdrawing a small amount of cash, late at night, two days after the boy's estimated death.

"After the fact," Hanley said, looking at the screen. "That's our timeline breach."

They didn't speak the word *motive* yet. In cases like this, motive was the luxury of hindsight. For now, they had proximity, movement, and opportunity.

Priya highlighted the overlapping data sets: phone pings, vehicle sightings, motel check-ins. "She didn't do this alone," she said. "Too many logistics for one person afraid and running. Someone helped her."

Hanley nodded. "Let's find her circle."

The Helpers and the Geography of Guilt

The woman's digital residue was slim but consistent. Venmo logs empty. No tax record for the past two years. Yet the prepaid card she'd used for motel rooms occasionally received small deposits from another account—one tied to a man named Eli Burns, a long-haul trucker with a history of unpaid child support and two suspended licenses.

"Burns worked the corridor," Priya said. "His routes match three of her phone pings. He's our courier or our lookout."

Detectives tracked him down at a truck stop outside Memphis. His rig smelled of diesel and denial.

"We're not here to talk about freight," Hanley said. "We're here about the suitcase."

Burns froze.

For three hours, they walked him through the map—where he'd been, where she'd been, how their routes kissed along the interstates. By the end, his hands shook too hard to light a cigarette.

"She said she was in trouble," he whispered. "I didn't ask what she was carrying."

"But you helped her load it."

He nodded. "She said it was clothes."

That confession broke the geography open.

Burns's GPS showed an unscheduled stop behind an old complex in rural Georgia. Deputies found what she hadn't erased: a storage-unit key, a toy car, paperwork with two surnames.

Inside the unit—children's clothes, small shoes, a backpack with a school tag. A folded report card marked *Kindergarten.*

"I can read my name," the boy had written.

Patterns of Neglect

Back in Indiana, the team met with a child-welfare liaison. Records showed years of short-term guardianships, missed checkups, abrupt relocations.

"The system saw him," the liaison said. "Just not all at once."

Administrative neglect hovered like a verdict. Nobody's crime. Everyone's failure.

"He didn't disappear the day he died," Vega said quietly. "He disappeared a little more every year."

Burns's cooperation led to another voice. Tara Holt, a former roommate, spoke without prompting.

"She said she couldn't handle him anymore. Said the crying got inside her head."

"Did she hurt him?"

"I never saw that. But she locked herself away. A month before she left, she sold his winter coat."

The terrain sharpened—not proof, but erosion. The long slide before collapse.

The Net Draws Closed

Priya surfaced one final detail. "She used a false ID at the motel—but her real birthday."

"Why?" Hanley asked.

"Because she didn't think it mattered anymore."

The birthday tied to a dormant family court file. A custody case abandoned midstream. The boy's biological mother had lost rights years earlier.

The warrant stack grew thick. Extradition requests. Financial subpoenas. An arrest order sealed in a judge's chamber.

The suspect didn't ask for a lawyer until the word *homicide* was spoken.

Rain lashed the courthouse windows as they waited.

"You think she ever loved him?" Hanley asked.

"Maybe once," Vega said. "But love without responsibility isn't love. It's nostalgia."

The next morning, the storage unit yielded more: photos, birthdays, playgrounds. A letter in a child's uneven scrawl:

Dear Mommy, I will be good now. Please don't cry.

"That's the voice she couldn't erase," Vega said.

The Closing Circle

Within seventy-two hours, charges were filed. Headlines followed. The boy's name spread across screens, carried by strangers who never knew him.

For investigators, there was no triumph—only a quiet relief shaped like exhaustion.

"We did our part," Hanley said.

"Now it's the court's turn."

In the final debrief, the prosecutor thanked them. "Without your reconstruction, this case would still be open."

"It wasn't reconstruction," Priya said. "It was listening."

Outside, the storm had passed. Vega stood before the board one last time. The photos and maps were just paper now, but together they told the full arc of a life.

"You can rest now," she whispered.

She pulled the final pin.

The circle was complete.

CHAPTER 8 THE TRIAL BEGINS

When Justice Waits Its Turn

Justice, when it finally arrives, doesn't stride. It shuffles in on motions and continuances, on chain-of-custody hearings and calendars rearranged by a judge with three other dockets. It enters quietly, sits in the second row, and waits to be called.

The Jury Is Chosen

Prospective jurors filled the pew-like benches—teachers and retirees, a nurse who worked nights, a warehouse manager with forearms like anchor chain. They were asked the ritual questions: Could you follow the law? Could you look at photographs you would rather not see? Could you decide a stranger's fate without letting sympathy or anger stand in for proof?

One woman dabbed her eyes when the prosecutor mentioned "a child victim." The judge's voice softened but did not bend. "Can you be fair?"

The woman took a breath, then nodded. "I can try," she said, and the court accepted trying as the oath it must often be.

By afternoon, twelve seats were filled and two alternates sworn. No one looked at the defendant longer than necessary. The room had already learned that looking makes it harder to be a mirror for the law.

Proof Versus Grief

The prosecutor stood, buttoned jacket, and began without theatrics. "This case," she said, "is about time. The time a boy needed air and did not receive it. The time adults chose concealment over help. The time it took investigators to give him back his name." She promised the jury clean lanes: forensics, digital evidence, eyewitnesses, chain of custody. "You will see a suitcase," she said. "You will hear from a doctor. And you will hear, in the defendants' own actions, the sound of guilt."

The defense followed, a measured baritone. "Tragedy is not the same as murder," he said. "Accidents happen. Panic happens. People make terrible choices after the fact that are not the same as causing a death." He warned about gaps: no video of the act itself, no confession to intent, alternate explanations for pathology. He asked the jury to hold the State to proof, "not to grief."

The words hung between them—proof and grief—like two weights waiting for a scale.

Before the first witness, the defense renewed a motion to suppress the doorbell footage and portions of the cell-site location data, citing Fourth Amendment concerns. The judge heard arguments with the calm of someone who had read the briefs twice.

"Private homeowners turned over their footage voluntarily," the prosecutor said. "And the cell-site data were obtained by warrant."

The defense pressed. "The geofence was overbroad."

The judge ruled from the bench: doorbell footage admissible, cell-site data within warrant scope, and any disputes about inference to be argued to the jury. "Motion denied," she said, and the trial took its first irreversible step forward.

Witnesses and Objects That Speak

Analyst Priya Rao testified first, the cartographer of digital air. She explained pings without condescension, let the maps do most of the talking. Colored dots marched across a projected screen— Georgia, Alabama, Kentucky, Indiana—each one anchored by time stamps and tower IDs. She showed how the prepaid phone slept in places where cameras later saw the woman and the blue suitcase, how it woke at 2:13 a.m. near a motel that smelled of cleaner, how it breathed again at the on-ramp two hours before dawn.

The defense cross-examined politely, then pressed: "You can't say with certainty who was holding the phone."

"No," Priya said. "But I can say where it was and when, and show you the footage that meets it there."

On redirect, the prosecutor asked, "If the data and videos are puzzle pieces, Ms. Rao, do they fit?"

"They fit," Priya said simply.

Eli Burns looked smaller in a suit jacket that belonged to a different man. He kept his eyes on the rail of the witness box as he admitted he'd helped load the suitcase into his trailer. "I didn't know," he said. "I swear to God I didn't."

"Why did you help?" the prosecutor asked.

"She said she was in trouble. I thought—" He swallowed. "I didn't think. That's the truth."

The defense tried to make him the center of suspicion. "You were paid, weren't you? Cash?"

"No."

"You didn't look because you were afraid you'd see a crime you were part of."

"I didn't look because I was a coward," Burns said, and the room believed him in a way that helped the State more than any hostility would have.

A housekeeper with practiced hands described a room that wouldn't come clean. "Like pine and something I won't forget," she said softly. "We had to air it out two days."

The manager authenticated records. The security technician authenticated the corrupted video the lab had partially restored: the boy and the woman in the hall, a timestamp that married the phone's ping. The chain-of-custody officer walked the jury through a monotone liturgy of seals and signatures—what was collected, by whom, when, and how it was stored.

The defense repeated its refrain: the video was grainy, the angle imperfect, the metadata not a face. "Your eyes could be mistaken," counsel said.

"Maybe," the technician conceded. "But the computer isn't."

The blue hard-shell case sat on a rolling cart like a relic. The forensic tech, Elena Morrow, outlined her process: photographs, swabs, microtubes, soil sampled from beneath the wheels, adhesive residue under ultraviolet light, the tiny tear in the lining that hid a half-burned receipt. She never raised her voice and never guessed.

"What did the barcode residue suggest?" the prosecutor asked.

"That the case had once borne a tag with ATL in the string—likely Atlanta."

"What did you find in the wheel housing?"

"Red clay and quartz consistent with soil common to portions of Georgia and Alabama."

"And inside?"

"Fibers consistent with motel-grade cotton sheets and blue strands matching the lining. Trace signatures of industrial cleaning agents—surfactants typical of bulk cleaners supplied to motels in that corridor."

The defense objected to "match" as overstating. Sustained. The tech corrected herself—"consistent with"—and the jury saw the difference between science and story: science is careful even when the story begs to sprint.

Dr. Elaine Porter spoke last that day. She didn't bring the photos up first; she brought vocabulary, translated. Hypoxia. Pulmonary edema. Cerebral swelling. "The findings are consistent," she said, "with asphyxial death."

The prosecutor took her through the anatomy gently, stopping at each threshold so the jury could see without falling in. When the images did appear, they were clinical, labeled, and brief. The room breathed as one organism—the collective exhale when the screen went dark.

On cross, the defense did what defense must. "Doctor, there are conditions—viral, metabolic—that can resemble some of these findings?"

"Some, yes."

"And time-of-death ranges are estimates, not certainties."

"Yes."

"And you cannot tell this jury the precise mechanism—hand, pillow, circumstance—that deprived this child of air."

"I can tell the jury," Porter said evenly, "that a living child was not provided emergent care, and was concealed after death. In my medical opinion, this is homicide."

The answer sat in the room like a stone in a river, the arguments for current to flow around later.

The Defendant Takes the Stand

The woman chose to testify. Defendants do, sometimes, when the story they've built in their heads needs oxygen even if it's thin at altitude.

Her voice was flat at first, then climbed as she reached for a script the facts wouldn't hold. "He fell asleep," she said. "I thought he was fine. When he didn't wake up, I panicked. I cleaned because I was scared. I left because I didn't know what else to do."

The prosecutor's questions were unhurried. "You didn't call 911."

"No."

"You purchased a strong cleaner."

"Yes."

"You transported a child's body across state lines in a suitcase."

Tears. "I was afraid."

"And when you were afraid, you chose yourself," the prosecutor said, not unkindly. "Not him."

On cross, the defense tried to rebuild intent as absence—no prior felonies, no history of overt violence. "You loved him," counsel prompted.

"I did," she said, and for a heartbeat the room strained to hear if love could sound like anything but a plea.

The State called one rebuttal witness: the landlord from Louisville. He spoke about bubbles and a dinosaur. "He was a sweet thing," the man said again, and the phrase—repeated word for word from the investigative phase—landed now like testimony from the life itself, not just the case.

Verdict and Aftermath

The judge read the law the way a map is read—this road for knowing, this road for doubt. She defined homicide, explained causation, cautioned against sympathy and prejudice, and returned always to the standard: beyond a reasonable doubt, not beyond all possible doubt. She gave them lesser-included offenses, the safety valves juries use to calibrate culpability when the human heart wants gradients.

"Deliberate slowly," she finished. "Deliberate together."

The courthouse fell into its peculiar silence. Lawyers pretended to work. Detectives paced. Families held hands too tightly. Rain stippled the parking lot outside the window.

A note came from the jury room. Then another. Then the quiet knock.

The jurors returned. The clerk read the verdicts. Guilty. Guilty. Guilty.

The room didn't gasp. It exhaled.

Vega felt the verdict like weather changing—not sun, not storm, just a pressure shift. Outside, rain eased to mist. At the roadside memorial miles away, pinwheels turned in a wind that had crossed state lines to be there, spinning for a boy who would now be carried in sentences that began with his name and ended with the word **remembered**.

CHAPTER 9 INSIDE THE HOME

Where Truth Still Lives

Some truths aren't found in evidence rooms or courtroom exhibits.

They live in the corners of places where people once tried to build ordinary lives—the chipped doorway paint, the wall where a height was once marked, the faded curtains that caught the last light before everything went wrong.

The House That Remembered

Two weeks after the verdict, Detective Vega found herself standing in front of a small yellow house in Georgia. It had been cleared, cleaned, and listed for rent again, but she had one last piece of work to finish: a supplemental report on the environment of the child's final months.

She unlocked the door and stepped inside. The air had that sterile smell of new paint covering old memory.

She didn't bring a camera. She didn't need one. Every mark, every sound, seemed to tell its own story.

The living room was bare except for the outline on the carpet where a couch once stood. Near the window, sunlight caught a single sticker still clinging to the glass—a smiling cartoon dinosaur, half peeled.

She noted it in her pad: Window decal. Child height. Facing east.

Sometimes, the smallest details said the most.

The People Who Saw Pieces

The landlord, Mr. Graves, met her in the driveway. He was an older man who'd spent his life collecting keys and stories he didn't want.

"She was always behind," he said, referring to the tenant—the woman now serving life without parole. "Paid late, promised to catch up. You could tell she was tired, but I didn't ask questions. I've learned not to."

He rubbed the back of his neck. "That boy—quiet kid. Never saw him play outside. Once, I gave him a lollipop when they came by to drop rent. He said thank you like it was a word he had to borrow."

Vega wrote down every word. Later, she would highlight the part about the silence. Quiet children often speak loudest in hindsight.

Next door lived the Hendersons—retired couple, lifelong residents of the neighborhood.

"She kept to herself," Mrs. Henderson said, pouring tea she didn't drink. "Sometimes we'd hear yelling. Not the angry kind—more like panic. Then quiet again."

Her husband added, "We offered to help once, when her car wouldn't start. She said no. Said she was fine."

The refrain echoed through so many interviews—I'm fine.

The phrase was a mask society often accepts at face value because it's easier than what might come next.

Mrs. Henderson pointed toward the small patch of lawn between their driveways. "He used to line up little rocks there," she said. "In rows. Every day, same number, different order. Maybe his way of making sense of things."

Vega could picture it: the boy kneeling in the grass, arranging his tiny world, creating order where there was none inside.

The Paper Trail That Thinned

The old case files had survived in a digital archive—brief summaries of visits, checklists of safety indicators, nothing overtly alarming. But between the lines, the slow fade was clear.

May 14: Home tidy. Child shy but responsive.

September 3: Missed medical appointment. Caregiver reports stress due to financial pressure.

January 8: Follow-up requested, contact not made.

And then nothing. No further entries.

In her report, Vega wrote:

"Systemic fatigue evident. Repeated missed connections between social services and the family. No single failure catastrophic, but cumulative neglect allowed conditions to deteriorate unseen."

She paused, staring at the cursor blinking after that sentence. It was easy to write systemic fatigue. Harder to admit what it meant: people too overworked, too under-resourced, too used to triaging crises to see the ones that bloom quietly behind closed doors.

The local elementary school still had a few staff who remembered the boy. One of them, Ms. Carter, had taught his kindergarten class. She kept an old class photo taped to the back of a filing cabinet.

"There he is," she said, pointing to the second row. "He never smiled for pictures. But he loved dinosaurs. Could name them all. Knew which ones were herbivores."

She hesitated. "He stopped coming halfway through the year. I called once, but the number didn't work. We have procedures, but... once they withdraw, we just mark it down."

She folded the picture carefully, as if the act of preservation were an apology. "I still keep him there," she said. "So he's not just a headline."

Vega thought of the hundreds of teachers across the country who carried similar ghosts—children they couldn't save, names they couldn't forget.

The Room Where He Lived

Back in the house, Vega stepped into what had been the boy's room. The space was empty, but faint outlines remained—lighter squares on the wall where posters had once hung, a small dent where a bedframe had pressed too long against plaster.

In the corner, she found a single screw in the floorboards. She pocketed it without knowing why.

Her mind replayed what the forensic team had described: the pattern of neglect, the quiet escalation of chaos, the weeks where survival overtook affection.

There were no monsters here—only exhaustion, shame, and silence metastasizing into tragedy.

From the evidence archives came a box labeled Miscellaneous Correspondence. Inside were letters written but never sent. Crayon on ruled paper. Some incomplete, some folded into odd shapes.

Dear Mommy, I learned to count to a hundred.

Dear Mommy, I saw a bird build a nest. Maybe we can build one too.

Dear Mommy, when I wake up, I will be good.

The handwriting grew smaller with each page, as though the writer were shrinking into himself.

Vega didn't cry. She'd learned that emotion, in her work, came like lightning—unexpected and dangerous if you didn't ground it. Instead, she whispered, "I hear you," and slipped the letters back into the box.

What Remains After the Case Closes

In her report to the task-force board, Vega didn't dwell on the crime itself. That part had been proven in court. She wrote instead about preventability. About how a dozen small failures had lined up like dominoes, and once the first fell, the rest never had a chance to stand.

She wrote:

"We often say 'no one could have known.' But the truth is, many knew pieces. The tragedy was not ignorance—it was fragmentation."

The board would later cite her report in a training program for cross-agency communication. But in her heart, Vega knew the changes would come too late for him. They always did.

Before leaving town, Vega stopped once more at the small memorial near the woods—the place where the suitcase had been found.

The flowers were wilted now, the stuffed animals bleached by rain. Someone had replaced the wooden cross with a metal plaque bearing the boy's full name, newly restored.

She knelt and placed the screw from the bedroom beside it. A tiny offering from the life he'd lived before the headlines.

"I hope you know," she whispered, "you mattered."

Back at her desk, Vega closed her final file on the case. She didn't print it. Paper would yellow; pixels would last.

She added one last note:

"The boy's case redefined local protocols for at-risk children. His life continues to speak in the form of new safeguards, new vigilance, and renewed empathy. His absence changed policy. His memory changed people."

She hit save.

Outside, evening light spilled across the precinct parking lot. The world went on, as it always does—but a quiet resolve lingered in the air, the kind that keeps certain hearts from forgetting.

For Detective Vega, that was justice enough.

CHAPTER 10
AFTERMATH
AND LEGACY

The Echo in Policy

Time does not erase tragedy; it weaves it into the fabric of memory. The case of the boy in the suitcase didn't simply end with a verdict—it began a long conversation about how a child can vanish in plain sight and how communities choose to respond when one does.

Six months after the sentencing, the state legislature convened an emergency review of child welfare oversight. The hearing room was filled not with cameras but with binders—pages of testimony, statistics, procedural failures laid bare.

Detective Vega sat in the back row, civilian clothes now, watching social workers and lawyers speak about reforms. Some came defensive, others trembling with regret.

A senator read from Vega's final report.

"The tragedy was not ignorance—it was fragmentation."

Those words became the heart of the new **Interagency Child Safety Initiative**, a law requiring unified databases, shared alerts between school districts and welfare departments, and mandatory follow-ups after withdrawal from public education.

It was slow work—bureaucracy always is—but for once, it moved. Not out of politics, but out of conscience.

The People Who Stayed

Priya stayed on the task force, promoted to lead digital forensics. She trained new analysts to look not just at data points, but at *patterns of silence*—those long stretches when a person disappears from the online grid. "Absence can be evidence," she told her trainees.

Hanley retired six months after the trial. His badge went into a drawer, but the case never left his mind. On some nights, he'd drive past playgrounds and listen to the laughter, making sure it still sounded like life.

Elena Morrow, the forensic tech who had testified about the suitcase, transferred to teaching. Her first lecture opened with a single slide: *Every object tells a story. Your job is to listen without judgment.*

And Vega—she stayed a detective, though she turned down promotion twice. She said her work wasn't finished yet.

The Memorial Garden

A year after the verdict, the small town near the discovery site built a memorial garden beside the community center. Volunteers planted rows of blue hydrangeas—the same color as the suitcase. At its center stood a bronze sculpture of a boy holding a bird in his hands.

The plaque beneath read:

In memory of every child who was not found in time.

May your stories teach us to see.

Families came to visit, leaving toys and flowers. Teachers brought students to talk about kindness, empathy, and what it means to notice when someone disappears from class.

For many, it became a sacred space—not of mourning, but of vigilance.

The Letters

The case's emotional wake was wide and unpredictable. Vega began receiving letters—some from strangers, others from parents who'd lost children in different ways. One stood out:

Detective Vega, I wanted you to know that I started volunteering with our local foster program because of what I read about your case. I can't change what happened to that little boy, but I can be one more person watching, listening, noticing. Thank you for reminding us that love can be a form of prevention.

Vega kept that letter pinned above her desk. On the hardest days, it reminded her why the job mattered—not for the arrests, but for the awakenings.

The Documentary

Two years later, a small independent film crew approached the department about creating a documentary. Vega hesitated, fearing exploitation. But when she read the proposal, she agreed. The film wouldn't dramatize; it would *educate*.

The director's goal was simple: to show how systems fail quietly, and how individuals could stop the fall.

When the film premiered at a regional festival, it ended not with sirens or headlines but with still photographs of the boy's memorial garden and a single sentence:

He was found because people refused to stop listening.

It won no major awards, but teachers began showing it in classrooms, and police academies added it to ethics courses. The story had found a second life—not as tragedy, but as a tool for compassion.

The Visit

One quiet spring morning, Vega returned to the memorial garden. The air smelled of rain and freshly turned soil. A group of schoolchildren were there, guided by a young teacher who told them about "the boy who helped change the law."

She watched them lay down paper cranes near the statue.

One girl, maybe six years old, turned to her and asked, "Were you there when they found him?"

Vega hesitated, then knelt down. "Yes," she said softly.

"Did it make you sad?"

"Yes," Vega said again. "But it also made me want to make sure it never happens to anyone else."

The girl nodded as if this were a promise she could carry. Then she ran off to join the others, her laughter breaking through the solemnity like sunlight through clouds.

The Annual Vigil

Every April, the community held a candlelight vigil near the site where the suitcase had once been found. Reporters stopped coming after the second year, but the people stayed—teachers, detectives, parents, survivors.

They didn't speak much. They didn't need to. The light spoke for them.

Each flame reflected in the small plaque's metal surface, making it appear as though the boy's name was glowing. For a few hours each year, his story was not about the way he died, but about the way he continues to change lives.

The New Detective

On her last day before transferring to the department's community-outreach division, Vega met her replacement—a rookie named Alicia Torres, bright-eyed and earnest.

"You worked that case," Alicia said quietly. "The suitcase boy?"

Vega nodded.

"What was the hardest part?"

"Realizing it wasn't just about one child," Vega said. "It was about how many we lose to silence."

Alicia wrote that down in her notebook. Vega smiled. "Don't write it like a quote," she said. "Write it like a reminder."

The Closing File

Years later, when the archives digitized old cases, an analyst noticed a marginal note on the file cover of the boy's case: *Closed, but never forgotten.*

No one could confirm who wrote it.

But that note became the unofficial motto for the new Missing and Endangered Child Task Force—a multidisciplinary unit that combined local, federal, and digital resources. Its first training session began with Vega's report as the founding document.

In the margins of that report, she had written in her own hand:

"Justice is not closure. Justice is continuity."

The Wind and the Field

Five years after the case, the field along Spurgeon Road looked almost ordinary again. The tall grass had grown over the tire tracks. Birds nested in the nearby trees. Only those who knew the story could point to the exact spot where everything had changed.

Vega sometimes drove by, not to remember the pain, but to measure how far the world had come since that morning.

As she stepped out of her car, a breeze lifted through the field, stirring the wildflowers. For a brief moment, she imagined the sound of a child's laughter carried on the wind—soft, distant, but unmistakably alive.

She smiled, whispered, "You're free now," and walked back toward her car.

The road that had once kept a secret now carried a legacy.

A story of a boy whose life, though brief, taught a nation to see the invisible, to listen harder, and to care before it's too late.

EPILOGUE

— The Weight of Remembering

Some stories stay with you not because of how they end, but because of what they reveal about who we are when no one is watching.

The boy in the suitcase was never just one child. He became the mirror in which a society had to look at itself—every broken promise, every unchecked silence, every time someone said "not my business" and turned away. His story was tragedy, yes, but it was also testimony. It testified to how neglect is born not only in violent acts, but in the slow erosion of care.

When I began writing this book, I didn't want to tell another story about a child lost. I wanted to tell a story about a world waking up —one detective, one teacher, one neighbor, one reader at a time.

Because behind every headline is a home that once held laughter. Behind every courtroom verdict is a chain of small choices that could have rewritten the ending.

In the years since his death, the boy's name has become a kind of prayer whispered in classrooms, caseworker trainings, and parent meetings. His legacy is not in the crime that ended his life, but in the vigilance that now protects others.

And still—there's the part of the story you can't legislate, can't digitize, can't quantify. The part that lingers in the heart.

It's the sound of a detective whispering to an empty room,

You mattered.

It's the teacher keeping a photograph taped to a file cabinet.

It's the stranger who reads about the case and decides to foster a child, or volunteer, or simply knock on a neighbor's door.

That is the quiet revolution of remembrance: not revenge, but renewal.

When we remember him, we are reminded that empathy is not weakness. It's the first line of defense.

So when you finish this book, I hope you don't close it with despair. I hope you close it with attention—with eyes a little sharper to see who might be fading at the edges of your world.

Because sometimes, saving a life isn't about grand gestures.

It's about noticing.

It's about asking the question before it's too late.

It's about caring enough to interrupt silence.

The boy in the suitcase is gone, but the lesson he left behind is not.

And maybe—just maybe—that's what justice truly looks like.

NEXT IN THE SERIES

The Children the World Missed

If this case haunted you, the next one will feel closer—and harder to look away from.

The Child No One Stopped: The True Crime Story of Damari Carter follows a boy who was seen, documented, and briefly noticed—yet still lost.

There were reports.
There were visits.
There were moments when intervention was possible.

And still, no one stopped what was happening.

This investigation traces how concern softened into delay, how warning signs lost urgency, and how a child can remain unprotected even while systems respond. It is not a story of disappearance—but of gradual erasure in plain sight.

Continue *The Children the World Missed* to confront the most difficult truth of all: sometimes the failure isn't that no one knew —it's that knowing wasn't enough.

 Tap here to continue to The Child No One Stopped: The True Crime Story of Damari Carter

Or scan the QR code to continue.

A PERSONAL REQUEST

Thank you for reading *The Boy in the Suitcase*: *An Investigative True Crime Novel.*

If this book resonated with you, I would be sincerely grateful if you chose to leave a review. Even a brief written comment— or simply selecting a star rating—makes a meaningful difference. Reviews help bookstores and reading platforms recognize that this story matters and deserves continued visibility.

If you would like to leave a review, you can visit the book's Amazon page here:*The Boy in the Suitcase: An Investigative True Crime Novel*

You may also scan the QR code on the following page to go directly to the review section.

Your support helps ensure that this story—and the lives at the center of it—are not forgotten.

With gratitude,

Linda Davidson

ALSO BY LINDA DAVIDSON

With Its Victims

ABOUT THE AUTHOR

Linda Davidson is a true crime author who writes for readers who want more than shock value — they want truth with a heartbeat.

She focuses on the kinds of stories that stay with you long after the news cameras leave: unsolved murders, missing persons, rural disappearances, and investigations that never received clear answers. Instead of chasing sensational headlines, Linda writes with one question in mind: *How can I honor the victim and still tell the full truth of what happened?*

In each book, she blends careful research, clear timelines, and compassionate storytelling. Readers are guided through evidence, leads, theories, and dead ends in a way that is easy to follow and emotionally grounded. Her work keeps the victim at the center of the narrative while also examining the failures, gaps, and human decisions that shaped each case.

Linda's books are written for true crime readers who care about people, not just plot twists. She writes for those who feel frustrated by shallow coverage and are hungry for deeper, more thoughtful explorations of the cases that haunt them.

Her promise is simple:

She will research carefully.

She will explain clearly.

She will tell the truth with respect.

She will never forget that the people she writes about were real.

Linda Davidson is a true crime author dedicated to telling the stories others forget. She writes about unsolved murders, mysterious disappearances, and cold cases with a focus on the victims, their families, and the communities left behind. Combining deep research with compassionate storytelling, she helps readers make sense of complex investigations without losing sight of the human beings at the center of every case.

About the Author

Linda Davidson is a true crime and historical nonfiction writer dedicated to uncovering stories that live in the shadows of history. With a background in research and a passion for justice, she writes with empathy for victims while exposing the human cost behind unsolved mysteries and infamous crimes.

Her mission is not to glorify criminals, but to restore dignity to lives cut short and to highlight the resilience of families who continue to seek answers. Blending meticulous research with vivid storytelling, Davidson brings forgotten stories to light and reminds readers that justice—though delayed or denied—is always worth pursuing.

END NOTE

— Light in the Dark

Stories like this one walk us through some of the darkest places a human heart can go. It is easy to believe that evil has the last word—that violence, corruption, or indifference are stronger than anything else.

The Bible says something different. It tells us that God sees every unseen hurt, hears every unheard prayer, and judges every hidden deed. It also says that no life is beyond His reach, and no story is too broken to be redeemed. Justice matters to God. So does mercy. So does you.

If what you've read has stirred fear, anger, or regret in your own heart, know this: the door back to Him is never closed. Repentance is simply turning around and letting Him meet you where you are.

"Do not be overcome by evil, but overcome evil with good."

— Romans 12:21

"The light shines in the darkness, and the darkness has not overcome it."

— John 1:5

May these pages not only expose what went wrong, but also awaken a hunger for what is right—for justice, for truth, and for the kind of grace that can still save a soul.

ETHICS ADDENDUM

- Why fictionalize? To prevent harm to living people while teaching investigative truth.
- What's changed? Names, dates, places, composite roles, and some sequences.
- What's faithful? Forensic processes, courtroom structure, policy failures, and the emotional reality of the work.
- Acknowledgments to Professionals (Template)
- Forensics & Pathology: [Names withheld / composites used].
- Law Enforcement: Task-force members who shared procedural insights.
- Child-Welfare Advocates: Trainers and frontline workers who reviewed drafts for sensitivity.
- Legal Review: Counsel who ensured ethical boundaries were preserved.

HELP & HELPLINES

International

- Child Helpline International — Finder for country-specific child helplines.
- National Center for Missing & Exploited Children (USA) — CyberTipline & resources.
- NSPCC (UK) — Helpline for child protection concerns.
- Kids Helpline (AU) — Counseling and crisis support for children/teens.
- Sweden
- SOS Alarm (Akut): 112 — Immediate danger.
- Polisen (Non-emergency): 114 14 — Child welfare concerns, advice, reports.
- 1177 Vårdguiden — Medical advice line.
- Socialtjänsten (Kommunal) — Local social services; report suspected child maltreatment.
- BRIS – Barnens Rätt i Samhället — Support for children/guardians (chat/phone).

Policy Notes & Reform Ideas (Toolbox)

- Unified Alerts: Automatic cross-notification between schools, healthcare, and social services on withdrawal/no-shows.
- Data Bridges: Limited, audited sharing of key risk flags (attendance, missed checkups) with child-welfare liaisons.
- Doorstep Protocols: When a child "disappears" from

public school, a welfare check within 10 business days.
- Community Training: Short courses for landlords, bus drivers, librarians on recognizing and reporting concerns.
- Digital Forensics MOUs: Pre-signed cooperation agreements with major doorbell/camera platforms for rapid lawful access.

PRACTICAL APPENDIX

If You're Worried About a Child

- **Notice:** sudden school withdrawal; chronic absences; isolation; visible fear; medical/dental neglect; persistent "we're fine" amid obvious distress.
- **Document:** dates, observations, what was said (verbatim when possible).
- **Report:** follow your country/state's mandated pathways. You **don't** need proof—reasonable concern is enough.
- **Follow up:** if safe, check back; systems miss calls—polite persistence saves lives.

READER & BOOK-CLUB GUIDE

(Discussion Questions)

- Where do you see "fragmentation" in real systems (schools, healthcare, social services), and how might those gaps be bridged?
- What responsibilities do bystanders and neighbors have when a child "goes quiet"?
- Did the fictionalization guardrails help or hinder your trust in the narrative? Why?
- Which investigative element (forensics, digital, eyewitness) most shifted your understanding of the case?
- What reforms from the book feel most actionable in your community?

GLOSSARY (QUICK REFERENCE)

- Asphyxia: Life-threatening lack of oxygen leading to organ failure.
- CFIT: Controlled Flight Into Terrain (aviation term; included for readers of author's broader work).
- CODIS / NamUs: US databases for DNA and missing/ unidentified persons.
- Geofence Warrant: Judicial order for anonymized device data within a defined area/time.
- Hypoxia: Reduced oxygen at the tissue level.
- Locard's Principle: Every contact leaves a trace.
- Manner of Death: Legal classification (homicide, accident, natural, suicide, undetermined).
- Toxicology: Testing bodily fluids/tissues for chemicals or drugs.

CASE TIMELINE (STORY WORLD)

- April 16 — Suitcase discovered on a rural road; scene secured.
- April 17–20 — Autopsy initiated; initial forensics on suitcase begin.
- May — Facial reconstruction released; nationwide tips surge.
- June–July — Phone pings, doorbell and traffic cameras narrow corridor.
- August — Storage-unit and motel evidence recovered; arrest warrants issued.
- Autumn — Arrests made; charges filed.
- Following Spring — Trial; conviction on primary and related counts.
- +6–12 months — Policy reviews; memorial established.

METHOD & SOURCES

This narrative is **fictionalized** to protect privacy while preserving procedural and forensic accuracy. Composite characters, altered timelines, and anonymized locations were used. Source base included: open-court records, publicly available agency manuals, forensic-pathology texts, policing standards, child-welfare policy documents, and practitioner interviews. A running bibliography is maintained separately and can be provided on request.

LEGAL NOTICE & DISCLAIMER

This book is a work of narrative nonfiction with elements of fictionalization. It is based on publicly available records, released investigative materials, court documents, archival reporting, and on-the-record statements. In places, scenes, dialogue, and narrative structure have been reconstructed or fictionalized to convey the substance of events where the public record is incomplete, contested, or ongoing. Every reasonable effort has been made to remain faithful to the known facts; however, errors or omissions may occur.

Some matters described remain unresolved, disputed, or subject to differing interpretations. Unless explicitly supported by official findings of a court or authorized investigative body, events and analyses should not be understood as adjudicated fact.

All individuals mentioned are presumed innocent unless and until proven guilty in a court of law. Allegations, theories, and suspicions are presented for historical and contextual purposes only and do not constitute assertions of guilt.

Analytical commentary and interpretation reflect the author's good-faith assessment of the available record and are presented as opinion based on cited sources.

In limited cases, nonessential identifying details may be withheld, altered, or composite characteristics employed to protect the privacy of private individuals and families. Such changes do not materially affect the narrative's intent or substance.

This book is not intended as legal, medical, psychological, or professional advice.

References to agencies, organizations, or institutions are for informational purposes only and do not imply endorsement or affiliation.

ACKNOWLEDGMENTS

This book exists because a great many people refused to let a child be forgotten.

I owe deep respect to the investigators—past and present—who worked this case with persistence, restraint, and professionalism. Many labored with limited tools, incomplete records, and little public recognition, yet continued to document, preserve, and question long after public attention moved on. Their commitment laid the groundwork for later breakthroughs and ensured that the record remained intact.

I am grateful to the journalists and researchers who reported on this case with care rather than sensationalism. Their contemporaneous reporting, archival diligence, and willingness to revisit uncomfortable truths made it possible to reconstruct events with accuracy and context. In particular, longform investigative work preserved details that would otherwise have been lost to time.

Special acknowledgment is owed to the forensic specialists and genealogists whose modern methods restored identity where none existed before. Their work represents not only scientific progress, but moral resolve—the belief that no case is too old, and no victim too small, to matter.

To the communities affected by this case, thank you for carrying its memory when there was no resolution to hold onto. Public remembrance, quiet advocacy, and decades of unanswered questions kept the pressure alive in ways official channels could not always sustain.

Finally, this book is written for the child at its center. He did not have a voice in life, and for far too long, he did not have a name. This work is offered in recognition of his humanity, and in the hope that careful telling can serve as a form of justice when so much else came too late.

Any errors or omissions remain my own.

AUTHOR'S NOTE

I did not set out to write a book about a suitcase. I set out to write about a child.

From the first whisper of this case, I felt the tension every true-crime writer knows: the public's right to understand versus a family's right to grieve; the urge to illuminate versus the risk of harm. This book walks that line with deliberate care. Though inspired by a real 2022 homicide, the narrative you've read is **fictionalized**: names, locations, timelines, and personal identifiers have been altered or composite-blended to protect privacy and to avoid interfering with ongoing or related legal matters. Where investigative procedures, forensics, or courtroom dynamics appear, they are presented accurately in spirit and practice, but never at the expense of a living person's safety or dignity.

Why tell it at all? Because stories shape attention—and attention saves lives. Children too often disappear not in a single moment, but through a slow fade of missed appointments, unanswered calls, moves without records, and the soothing lie of "we're fine." Writing this book was my way of refusing that fade. I wanted to show, with respect and restraint, how investigators listen to the "quiet evidence," how communities rally, and how systems can change when ordinary people refuse to look away.

My ethical guardrails were simple:

1. Center the child. Not the spectacle, not the defendants, not the author.
2. Do no gratuitous harm. No graphic details, no sensationalism, no voyeurism.

3. Protect the living. Composite characters, anonymized settings, and timeline shifts prevent identification.
4. Honor the work. Law enforcement, forensic teams, social workers, teachers, and neighbors are portrayed with realism: fallible, persistent, and—at their best—compassionate.
5. Offer a next step. A story should leave the reader with something to do.

If this book moved you, consider these quiet, practical actions: learn local reporting pathways for suspected abuse or neglect; support overburdened child-welfare nonprofits; show up at school board and council meetings where data-sharing and follow-up policies are shaped; ask about the children who suddenly "withdraw." Most of all, check on the families at the edges of your life—the ones who say they're fine when everything says otherwise.

To the professionals who shared best practices and to the survivors who trusted me with their wisdom: thank you. To readers who held this story gently—allowing it to change your attention without hardening your heart—thank you most of all.

This book is, in the end, a memorial of a different kind: not stone or bronze, but vigilance. May we carry the lesson forward—eyes open, voices ready, compassion intact.

— **Linda Davidson**

.

www.ingramcontent.com/pod-product-compliance
Ingram Content Group UK Ltd.
Pitfield, Milton Keynes, MK11 3LW, UK
UKHW020720110326

11196UKWH00015B/1336